ONE HUNDRED FILM HAIKU

THE REEL THING

Mick Haining

First published 2013 by IRON Press
5 Marden Terrace
Cullercoats
North Shields
NE30 4PD
tel/fax +44(0)191 2531901
ironpress@blueyonder.co.uk
www.ironpress.co.uk

ISBN 978-0-9565725-2-3
Printed by Field Print
Boldon on Tyne

© Mick Haining 2013

Typeset in 11pt Georgia
Book design and lay-out by
Brian Grogan & Peter Mortimer

IRON Press Books are distributed by Central Books
and represented by Inpress Ltd
Churchill House, 12 Mosley Street
Newcastle on Tyne, NE1 1DE
Tel: +44 (0) 191 2308104
www.inpressbooks.co.uk

Supported by
ARTS COUNCIL
ENGLAND

Foreword

I THINK MY FIRST HINT OF IMPERMANENCE CAME FROM
my mother. She used to get her hair 'permed'.
Once I'd found out that her wave was not
actually 'permanent', but needed occasional
re-doing, it may have planted the seed of this
preoccupation I have with the passing moment.
Eventually, I became a drama teacher, where
I could help students organise the passing
moments into representations of reality that
might help them understand what it's like to
be other humans in other places at other times.
And I've always loved the cinema. The films
I would watch would show 25 still images a
second, creating the illusion of movement.
Somewhere around 30 years ago, I came across
The Narrow Road to the Deep North by Basho.
It was interesting but not that earth-shaking
– I probably wasn't ready for it. Now I regret
that I no longer have it. It was when I began
to write plays for my students to perform that
I really had to consider the significance of
each passing moment - the weight of a word,
intonation, gesture or glance might be crucial
to creating perhaps unexpected understanding.

By now, I also had a garden to tend which at times seemed more concerned with teaching me about intransigence rather than impermanence. Illusion, impermanence, nature... I was ready for haiku now.

All art forms are as subject to transience as anything else, otherwise we'd still be painting Egyptian profiles or plainchant would be top of the download charts. Films are no longer silent and John Wayne has passed. So, reducing iconic films to a mere seventeen syllables seems a perfectly valid exercise to me and one which has given me plenty of fun. I just hope that you, the reader, get some of that fun, too.

Either read the film titles first or alternatively read the haiku first, then try to guess the film titles - two different experiences.

Mick Haining
Summer 2013

Biography

I WAS BORN AND REARED IN MOVILLE, CO. DONEGAL, where sea meets sky and land, a conjunction that broadcasts transience. The first film I was allowed to see at an evening performance without my mother was *The Cruel Sea*, a 1953 release with Jack Hawkins. I'm not sure if it was before or after that I painted a destroyer ploughing through choppy seas that won a prize at the local library. There was little competition. Eventually, I became a drama teacher. Years later, I wrote this haiku:

I stand on a rock
To watch a single wave break
And exist no more.

We are those waves. This book is a bit of mine. Now I 'create' haiku with materials which are in themselves transient, e.g., driftwood, leaves, holly berries, sand, barnacles, cat biscuits... I then photograph them before usually leaving them for nature to treat them as she pleases – in one case, her representative was a cat... ZigZag Publications are currently selling a couple of my efforts – *How to Get an A* in*

Drama, three plays and a collection of short plays based on ancient Greek myths. I've also written a collection of short stories set in the future when the ice caps have melted and England is an archipelago. Nobody's published them yet – I'll have to try harder.

One Hundred Film Haiku

God-fearing woman

And drunk captain find romance

And a German gunboat.

Blast-off routine check:

Air locks? Shut. Thrusters? Engaged.

Stowaway check? Oops.

The African Queen [1951]
Alien [1979]

The talk of the town,

Unwilling to change. At last,

He pays lip service.

They wore black to dine

But ate a sumptuous meal

In Technicolor.

Forward to the past!

Mum and Dad! You have to meet!

[It's perfectly tense!]

Une femme au foyer

Discovers prostitution

Is what rings her bell.

Back to the Future [1985]
Belle de Jour [1967]

11

The pecking order

Is reversed when birds attack.

What rattled their cage?

Nuns on the run from

Worldly pleasure fight desire.

Old habits die hard.

The Birds [1963]
Black Narcissus [1946]

Her life's ambition –

To be Swan Queen, but self-harm

Ruffled her feathers.

In the woods today,

You're sure of a big surprise –

It's not a picnic!

Och, whit dae we want?

To get rid o' Sassenachs.

Aye, or we'll be kilt

A speck in her eye

Provided the platform for

A tragic romance.

Ruthless ambition

Took him to the very top

But life's no sleighride.

A heady cocktail

Of politics and passion

Ends with a snakebite.

Citizen Kane [1941]
Cleopatra [1963]

15

Prison teaches him

That you can't break a record

Without boiling eggs.

Postcard from New York:

Sheilas are beaut. Tucker's fine.

In love. Fair dinkum.

It's the President!

We'll blast that comet for him!

Give him a big wave!

Four men in two boats

End up an unwholesome creek

Without a paddle.

Deep Impact [1998]
Deliverance [1972]

Magazine temp finds

Lies and double-crossing are

The height of fashion.

They went like lions,

But made monkeys of themselves

And were trapped like mice.

A troubled young man!

What his mind most needed was

A rabbit-proof fence.

Little red hoody?

You shouldn't go to Venice

But to Specsavers!

The taste of freedom

For motorbike hippies proves

Too much of a blast.

With a heart of gold,

His hands were of stainless steel –

A slice of bad luck!

Easy Rider [1969]
Edward Scissorhands [1990]

20

An innocent man

Wishes that everybody

Would stop bugging him.

You know me so well,

It's as if we've met before.

What's your name again?

She's so alluring

He betrays his marriage, but...

She's a bunny girl.

Please, please, darling! Please!

Don't mess with your DNA

Or else I'll swat you!

I do and I do.

I do and I do and then

I don't anymore.

'Small is beautiful'

Lies Cleo, but her evil

Is dwarfed by revenge.

It takes balls of steel

For men to become strippers.

Caps off to the five!

Hard Geordie goes home,

Drops rival at a car-park,

Has day at the beach.

She could throw a pot

But another medium

Was what she wanted.

Maximus reborn!

His growing success is deemed

Incommodious.

A headless horse, man!

No ghost tale nor Jane Austen.

It is persuasion...

Their relationship

Was passionate and stormy –

An uncivil war.

The Godfather [1972]
Gone With the Wind [1939]

Our sheriff's leaving.

Wait! He's coming back again!

Everybody, hide!

Grammar school students

Achieve places at Oxbridge

Having been Hectored.

High Noon [1952]
The History Boys [2006]

They are rescued by

A second-class citizen –

No reservations!

Puppies are stolen.

The crooks try to get away

But they are spotted.

Hombre [1967]
101 Dalmatians [1996]

Across frozen miles

A toddler is protected.

It's a mammoth task.

Rebels with a cause

Begin a cane mutiny

And fire down below.

Ice Age [2002]
If... [1968]

Whut you doin', boy,

With yo' fancy Northern ways?

Jus' solvin murdahs...

In the depths of sleep,

They try to alter his mind.

Do they fail? Dream on!

His dad sneezes and

The germ of an idea

Dooms the aliens.

Hmmm. That's curious.

The neighbours are not themselves.

Think I'll take a nap.

Achievements – solid.

Determination – solid.

Faculties – rusty.

Would-be warrior

With a Full Metal Jacket

Is his own Platoon!

They flee with the gold

But whether they've won or not

Is finely balanced.

Small town, big troubles

Drive him to the edge. He's back

In time for Christmas!

They tackled a shark,

Bit off more than they could chew

In a too-small boat.

Unprecedented,

Father and son exchange words.

The rest was silence.

They kill her bridegroom.

She survives and recovers.

Enter, dragoness!

He wasn't kidding

About his wish for stardom,

Only kidnapping.

Despite royalty,

The words 'I'm superior'

Were too hard to say.

Elderly woman

Kidnapped on a Balkan train.

It's just not cricket

The King's Speech [2010]
The Lady Vanishes [1938]

Nasty criminals

Could murder a cup of tea

But not its maker.

This has no dancing

And has nothing to do with

The price of butter.

The Ladykillers [1955]
Last Tango in Paris [1972]

Camel Diary:

Another scorcher. Long ride.

Captured Aqaba.

Musical trio

Turn up for daughter's wedding.

But who's the daddy?

"Plenty brave white man,

We make you one of us now."

"Hang on a minute..."

.gone memory's If

impossible almost Is

.murder a Solving

Rich kid learns the truth.

His city runs like clockwork,

Girfriend's a model...

A plot too clichéd?

To have the man you fancy,

You get him legless.

He drove her around.

She couldn't promise him much,

Not even a smile.

They capture the ship

And flee first to Tahiti,

Their futures Blighted.

Mona Lisa [1986]
Mutiny On the Bounty [1962]

41

Some brief encounters

Between teacher and student -

A bitter lesson!

He persuades his crew

To make one last fishing trip.

Hopes for a windfall.

She betrayed her man.

Five finger exercises

Now impossible.

A puppet's nose grows

Because he does not obey

The rules of Cricket.

Fleeing with the cash

She opts to take a shower –

It's curtains for her.

Of course, this should have

Just seventeen syllables,

But only five here.

That bandit killed him.

His wife did? No! Suicide!

Who... Oh, I give up!

Watching the neighbours,

He witnesses a murder

But he can't hop it!

Rashomon [1950]
Rear Window [1954]

45

Multi-coloured gang.

Diamond heist fails. Success pales

Beside treachery.

The Japanese 'prove'

That watching TV can be

Bad for you. Well, well!

Reservoir Dogs [1992]
Ringu [1998]

A struggling boxer

Discovers a new way of

Tenderising meat.

Killing each other,

Montagues and Capulets –

A Miami vice!

They murder a friend

And spin a plausible yarn

But stretch it too far.

Ninety-five minutes

Through thirty-five palace rooms

In a single shot!

Rope [1948]
Russian Ark [2002]

Such a waste of lives!

Did they even need to try

Saving Jason Bourne?

He can't see colour

But the veteran still likes

To paint the town red.

Even behind bars,

A convict's life is enhanced

By a poster girl.

Haunted by the dead,

Young Cole leads Malcolm to see

What he cannot see.

When he loses her,

He replaces his daughter

With a nip and tuck.

A childless woman

Reveals that she once had kids.

Sie waren Juden.

The Skin I Live In [2011]
Sophie's Choice [1982]

51

The hills are alive

With the threat of Nazi rule

But they are not Trapped.

Me! Me! Me! Me! Me!

Me! Me! Me! Me! Me! Me! Me!

Me! Me! Me! Me! Me!

A little princess

Shows she needs help. It can't be

A solo effort.

My plan, tennis star?

I'll kill yours if you kill mine.

Kind of mixed doubles.

Asking that question

Before the mirror, oh, yes!

We're lookin' at you!

Two friends on the run

Seem cornered by the police

But they just take off...

Taxi Driver [1976]
Thelma and Louise [1991]

He realises

That their love can't continue –

He puts her on ice.

To fund a friend's play,

He doctors his appearance.

He's a bosom pal!

Wannabe hotshot

Beds his flying instructor.

Yes, he's on her tail...

In a sleepy town

A good cop discovers that

All's well that ends Welles.

They're not unfeeling.

First chance of an adventure,

They're animated!

Drug and booze abuse

And lavatory humour

Take life down the pan.

Toy Story [1995]
Trainspotting [1996]

Boy gets his first car.

Seems old, but turns out to be

An automatic.

The reality

Became clear when he came up

To the horizon.

Transformers [2007]
The Truman Show [1998]

Gangs of New York make

A song and dance about it.

Look out! Shark attack!

They want the kittens

And their prayers seem answered

When they find Jesus.

Guns and religion

Don't go together as well

As a horse and trap.

The IRON Press haiku list

The small Japanese verse form haiku is slowly being assimilated into western literature and reaching areas beyond its traditional terms of reference.

We are the main independent book publishers of haiku in the UK. See our website for the full list. One recent example is shown below.

The Humours of Haiku

For anyone who thinks haiku arouse only a very narrow range of emotions, this anthology – with 240 haiku by over 100 poets — is a challenge to think again. Sadness, anger, jealousy, pity, compassion, regret and joy are just some of the emotions covered.

Price £7.00